Poop Tales

The Perfect Reading Material
for Any Bathroom

A Compilation of Hilarious Stories

Jeffrey Scott and Jeffery James

AuthorHouse™
1663 Liberty Drive, Suite 200
Bloomington, IN 47403
www.authorhouse.com
Phone: 1-800-839-8640

First published by AuthorHouse 01/20/09

ISBN: 978-1-4389-4213-1 (sc)

Printed in the United States of America
Bloomington, Indiana

Contents

Chapter 1

Why?

What on earth would possess someone, anyone, to actually write a book completely devoted to stories about crap? Sure, we've all read some crappy books, but few have been devoted to such a topic. The idea came to me following a trip back to my college town for a wedding of an old buddy. Ten years had passed since graduation, and I had maintained contact with about 10 of these guys. These are truly special friends since these are the people whom I first experienced life away from home with. During those four years of pseudo adulthood, we learned more about each other than our parents actually knew about us. In most cases, we learned much more than we really cared to.

I remember the drive to the wedding when my wife says to me, "you're not going to get drunk and embarrass me, are you?" Although I'm excited to see my old buddies, I do sympathize with her, knowing full well what happens every time alcohol and these old friends are mixed. A successful night out is a night of dancing without dropping my trousers to show off my boxers. She also anticipated the dreaded monotony of listening to the same old stupid stories that are only funny to those of us who were actually present at the time the stupidity occurred. It seems to be at these type of reunions, and only at these reunions, that you can hear a prominent attorney or an accomplished doctor say (while gleaming with pride) "remember when I got locked out of my dorm room and I was naked?" The laughter from the "old buddies" roars out as the wives take turns mustering up a smile as a courtesy to their idiotic husbands.

On this particular evening the storytellers started loosening up, as we all got liquored up. By 11:00 p.m. the stories start to become a little racier, and of course 11:00 to a married couple with children is equivalent to 2:30 a.m. in the old days. By this time even the wives began to find humor in some of the stories. The laughter attracted a few of the other guests who were able to identify with our memories from their own college days. The crowd accumulated to about 15 people including the bride and groom. The groom was one of our buddies from the old days, but he was cautious, not sure whether his new bride would approve of such humor, especially on her wedding night.

The topics ranged from hilarious pranks pulled on each other to foolish behavior that occurred after one of us had had too much to drink. These acts of stupidity were usually posted in the living room of our old apartment onto a giant poster board known as the "Wall of Shame." Suddenly the conversation traveled from R-Rated topics to a sharp turn passed the gutter, straight to the sewer. That was when my buddy known as Wilky began telling one of his "Poop" stories. He has shared these stories many times over, but never had I heard one among mixed company. Even with a strong beer buzz, I remember looking over at the bride and wondering if we were about to cross the line. It must have been the alcohol causing everyone at the table to be sick and demented like us, because everyone was laughing hysterically. One story spawned another until everyone was getting in on the action. Hell, my wife who had ordered me not to embarrass her even chimed in and said "oh Honey, you've gotta tell them what happened to you the other night!" The poop (stories) was flying and the crowd of listeners grew from table to table. The relatives of the bride were even listening to the contagious subject, and all kinds of people were sharing their most embarrassing moments.

On the ride home the following day, my wife and I were revisiting those tales and we continued to laugh all the way home. This dark humor may be disgusting to some, but the truth be told, we have all been there. From the sexiest, most beautiful woman in any glamour magazine, (who most believe has only used a bathroom for its mirror); to that big, fat, uncle guy who I suspect actually pooped his pants while laughing. This is to all of those wives who emphatically state, "You're disgusting, I would never call someone in to see that!" Yet, they knew full well what they were about to see, the minute they're husband called out "Hey, come in here and look at this!" So sit back, relax, flush and enjoy this compilation of stories, one sitting at a time as you read, no doubt, the most perfect reading material for any bathroom.

Chapter 2

Blocked

"Good night and thanks for everything," I tell my father as I am helping my three-year-old daughter into her car seat. My wife has already put our six-month-old daughter into her car seat and is starting up the car. On this particular evening, my wife and I drove separately and met each other at my parents' home, immediately following work. My beautiful wife and I have been married for three years and we are in our early thirties. I am about 5 feet, 11 inches tall and weigh about 200 pounds. Although I appear to be in decent physical shape when wearing a sweatshirt, I am comfortably hiding a slight pooch belly under the loose clothing. I am an ex-college wrestler who has developed atrocious eating habits over the years, which I attribute to the previous years of "making weight." For those not familiar with amateur wrestling, it was once commonplace for a wrestler to prepare for the up and coming match by starving himself down to the limit of the weight class, only to gorge oneself after the official weigh-in. I can remember on one occasion in which I gained 5 pounds in a matter of two hours, only to fast again the next week. Definitely not a pattern I condone now. This pattern has caused me to approach each meal as if it were to be my last. I can't stop eating until I feel stuffed. Although 10 years have passed since I wrestled last, my wife affectionately reminds me, "Jeez, slow down you pig, you can have more in an hour if you begin to melt."

We don't go to buffets anymore because I tend to take the "all you can eat slogan" a little too literally. I don't know how many times I've unbuttoned my pants for some comfort, only to go back one more time for a little soft serve ice cream with those wonderful toppings that everyone has been breathing over.

I am still saying good-bye to my parents as my wife and children are backing out of the driveway. A couple of minutes had passed since my wife had driven down the street and I begin to exit their driveway as well. As usual, I ate too much and I am as bloated as a road kill raccoon that has been baking in the sun for 10 hours. The first grumbling in my stomach reminds me that I probably shouldn't have chased down that third bowl of chili with that second piece of Key lime pie, followed with two cups of coffee. Those of you who do not drink coffee may be surprised to hear that not only does a nice, strong cup of java give you a caffeine kick-start to the day, but it also kick-starts most colons. Despite the persistent grumbling in my tummy, I decide to push forward for the 15-minute drive home. A short 5 minutes later however, the stirring turned to churning and the pressure began to build. I realized that I was beyond turning around and I began to disregard the speed limit. With every second, my stomach churned more and more. I'm not kidding, this was getting serious. My stomach felt like it was a pop bottle that had been shaken for 3 straight days and left in 90-degree heat. At this moment, the most important muscle in my body was no longer my heart, but my sphincter which was about to be put to the test. I was clenching the steering wheel with a death grip and a cold sweat was beading off my forehead. I've got about two minutes left in my journey and I seriously doubt that I'm going to make it.

Although my wife left a good 2 minutes ahead of me, I pulled into the driveway right behind her. Normally I would help the kids out of the car, but there is absolutely no time. As I do a butt-clinching run across our lawn to the front door, my wife only shakes her head in disgust. She has absolutely no sympathy for my predicament, as she has warned me to change my eating habits repeatedly. I catch a glimpse of my bewildered three year old daughter's face and faintly hear "why is Daddy running into the house, Mommy?" My wife's disgust is evident in her voice as she answers, "Daddy is potty training too, sweetie."

My hands felt like lobster claws as I simultaneously fumbled around with my keys and unbutton my pants at the front door of my home. I'm less than 10 seconds away from the most powerful release of my life, whether I'm in the bathroom or not. I can actually see that big, beautiful bowl down the hall. I can't help wonder if the fact that the lid is down will be the difference between sweet, unscathed relief or pure humiliation of being called "Mr. Poopy pants" by my wife for the rest of our marriage. In one complete and swift motion; I flip the lid, swing the rear around, and began to release the hounds in mid air. For that one instant I am feeling the greatest release of bodily tension that anyone on earth has ever felt. Normally, I would sit and savor such comfort; only to basque, twitch and shudder slightly from such a beautiful escape. Butt glory quickly turned to doom, as reality hits me like a sledge hammer. I suddenly am faced with the ugly truth that in the smooth, yet aggressive flip of the lid, it had ricocheted back and closed just underneath me as I went to sit down. A split second later, following the upside down volcanic blast, I felt as if a warm chocolate milk shake was being poured **up** my back. I slowly turned around and to my horror I see my own sludge on the walls and the base of the sink. Upon realizing what had just happened, a terrible stench crept up my nostrils. I hear knocks at the door and my daughter says "what's that smell Daddy?" She and my wife, both have weak stomachs and I can hear them gagging as they fight back the hurls.

I was literally stuck in there for close to an hour cleaning the bathroom and myself up. As I finally come out, my sweet little daughter offers me the only compassion I've heard all night and she says "its ok Daddy, I've pooped on myself before too."

Chapter 3

Kids Doo Too

This tale is about two young brothers who live with their single-parent mother. The elder brother, Kevin, is seven years old and is a perfectly well behaved, quiet little boy who is any teacher's dream student. Kevin's mother appreciates all the praise she receives from neighbors and teachers, but is also wise to his skillful techniques of antagonizing his hyperactive four-year-old brother, Jeff. Although Jeff always gets caught, he is not always the one who initiates the mischief. Jeff is a short, stocky little guy compared to his much taller, thinner, older brother. Their loving mother has placed her two boys above all else, often including herself. This devotion can take its toll on her patience and nerves, though. Mom's temper can flare up quite quickly and we both fear the swift hand that has found our bottoms on more than one occasion. Whenever one of us becomes sick or hurt, Mom's nurturing is second to none. Whenever we were caught trying to get away with something....well, let's just say whoever coined the phrase "tough love" must have been inspired by Mom. I can remember one time, when my brother tricked me into eating a giant spoonful of white paint. He said it was frosting, and being a chubby little guy, I was always hungry, so I dipped a big spoon into the can of paint and stuffed it into my mouth. Mom rushed in when she heard my screaming, after Kevin told me I was going to die of paint poisoning. She instantly gave each of us a bright red handprint on our bare legs. She then, tenderly, washed off my face and let me know that I'd be fine. "Why did you hit me too, Mom?" I asked when she was no longer angry. Mom pondered a second and answered, "Well, I was mad and you know you're not supposed to eat sweets before dinner." I guess she was right, we hadn't eaten dinner yet.

Although Kevin and I fought like cats and dogs, we spent most of our time together being silly and laughing at each other's antics. Saturday night bath time was no different. We were at that age, when we were old enough to take a bath without constant supervision, but young enough to take a bath together. On this particular night, Mom was on the phone with a girl friend, in the living room. She was in earshot of our frequent summons. "**Mom**, Kevin won't give me my G.I. Joe!" "**Maw-umm,** Jeff is splashing water on the floor!" "**Mawaw-ummm,** Kevin is trying to dunk my head under the water! "**Mawww-ummmm,** Jeff is using my wash cloth to wash his butt!" Mom storms in with a phone at her ear and yells: "listen boys; I'm on the phone and if I have to come in here again, neither of you will be able to sit for a week!" Neither of us knows how long a week is, but we both know that sitting involves our butts, so we straighten up immediately. Soon the threat is a faded memory to a couple of rambunctious little boys.

"Oooooh, those bubbles stink Kev!" "Do it again" I laughingly command. Bloop, Bloop, is followed by roars of laughter from both of us. "Watch this one," he says excitedly. Bloop....erreee.....bloop, causes hysterical laughter. Mom suddenly appears at the doorway to ask, "What are you boys doing in there?" Mom's face clearly indicates that she is not as amused as we are. "Nothing," we respond in unison. A scowl still on her face and a few seconds pass as she lingers before returning to the living room, obviously not buying the "nothing" response. As soon as we hear mom talking on the phone again, Kevin starts up. "Watch this one," he says eagerly. Nothing happens for a moment as I anxiously wait to see the bubbles, but as I look up I can't help noticing Kevin's face is turning beat red. Suddenly the silence is broken with "Bloooop...Ma aaaaawwwwwwuuuuuuummmmm!! **Kevin Pooooped!!!!**

I jumped out of the tub like I was struck by lightening and turned to face the action. Kevin, still in the tub, is using my washcloth to try and catch the elusive little brown buoy. All of a sudden I feel lightening strike my behind and hear the sound of Mom's hand on my little, bare bottom. This combination startles me so much, that I jumped up and landed back in the tub. As my brother and I panic, terrified that "it" will touch us, we begin flailing, which caused each of us to fall down before either of us can climb back out. The sight of the little piece of poop, infuriated Mom as she yelled "that's disgusting, you filthy little beasts!" She yanked my brother out of the tub by the arm and proceeded to do the unthinkable. Mom reached in with her bare hand and grabbed the little turd, tossing it into the toilet. The horrific sight caused my brother and me to simultaneously say "ooooh, gross!"

Of course, our outburst led to another swat. Needless to say, this incident ended our baths together forever.

Chapter 4

Another Kid's Tale: Wipe Out

As an adult, I pay little attention to the mundane, reflexive task of wiping after taking care of business. Certainly, I can appreciate individual styles, such as those who choose to neatly fold the toilet paper into several layers of squares, compared to others who prefer to haphazardly wad the paper into a big ball. Although the latter is a bit more crude, the thickness of the paper definitely wards off the dreaded finger puncture, when too few layers are used during the neatly folded technique. Sure you may save a few pennies on toilet paper over the long haul, but I dare question the risk to reward analysis. Some people choose to reach around and swipe, others go between the legs, and some prefer to stand. Each person's method becomes automatic, with very little thought once established, unless of course you have children. The automatic task is suddenly mulled over in thought as a father thinks to himself: "How the hell do I teach my son to wipe his own butt?"

I've always used the folding method followed by a minimum of two swipes, repeating as necessary. This, however, is far too complicated for my three-year old son to master. So, I've given in and allow him to just wad up the paper and wipe. Although this method is much easier for him, he uses far too much paper, giving me a great appreciation for the inventor of the plunger.

Anyone familiar with the "terrible two's", knows all too well that the single most challenging characteristic of this phase of growing up is the battle for independence. In my son's efforts to reach independence, he insists that I leave him alone while he goes to the bathroom, so as to prove that he can take care of business all by himself. I still check in on him after he is finished to make sure he was able to do a thorough job of clean up. Usually, he is unable to get all of the poop off, so I must finish the job. That is why, the next time he called me into the bathroom, I was already rolling up my sleeves as relief wiper. My son was emphatically yelling, "I did it Dad, I really did it!" To my joyous surprise, he was as clean as he could be. We celebrated with high fives, sang a little song, and did a little dance. He pulled up his pants and pulled down his shirt. I then told him to go and tell mom all about it. As he ran down the hall, I just didn't have the heart to rain on his parade by telling him about the giant skid marks all over the back of his shirt, which must have gotten in the way while he was wiping so well. *We'll let mom be the monsoon*, I thought to myself. I guess I learned three lessons that day: 1) just because he will grow into it someday, isn't a good enough reason to buy a shirt that is too big for a potty trainer, 2) cotton shirts do make great toilet paper in a pinch, and 3) the Seinfeld character George Castanza is smarter than I thought.

Chapter 5

Big Kids

(The college years)

Spring Break, most likely, brings back many fond memories for a lot of people about wild partying, hot chicks (or dudes), new romances and great poop stories. What? No **poop** stories? Well, let me share a few of mine. It was my junior year of college and I had finally saved up enough money to go on spring break (actually, some idiotic company gave me a credit card, what fools!). Four buddies and I were heading off to South Padre Island. We decided to go there, because one of the guys had grandparents who lived a little more than an hour drive away from the island. Although we weren't thrilled about crashing at his grandparents' house for Spring Break, none of us could afford to rent a condo for a week.

Actually, his grandparents turned out to be really cool and they were great hosts. They let us come and go as we pleased, and they seemed to enjoy hearing about our adventures from the previous night. The biggest downfall was the drive, which we usually made twice a day. We would typically drive to the island in the morning; hang out at the beach, drive back to clean up, and then drive back to the island for the night life.

The two weeks before we left for Padre Island, I had gone into a spring break training so-to-speak, in which I had purposely cut down my food intake, so that when we were on break, my body wouldn't require as much food. That way, I could spend less money on food and more on beer! (Solid guy reasoning!) This worked out great financially, but it wasn't so good to my intestinal system.

The first day that we drove to the Island from my buddy's grandparent's house, we had gotten a late start and arrived at the beach at about 5:00 in the afternoon. We found a place to park near some condos where we could just sit, drink beer and watch girls walk by. After several hours of that, I felt a rumbling feeling in the pit of my stomach. I ignored it for as long as I could, but eventually realized it wasn't going away. Since we weren't staying on the island, I really had nowhere to go. As the pressure continued to build, I spotted groups of people hanging out on the patios of several ground floor condos. I could only hope to see someone who might be understanding of my situation and have enough compassion to let me use their facilities. I told my friends my plan of action, and amid their laughter and harassment, I spotted a room that had three average looking guys in it. I walked over to the guys and explained my predicament, emphasizing my ever-pressing need to use their restroom. To my surprise, they were quite compassionate and agreed to let me use their restroom, as soon as their girlfriends came out. **Girls**, I hadn't seen any **Girls**. Telling the fellas I had to take a dump was one thing, but revealing this human need to **girls** was totally different. "*Oh No!*, I thought, as I could feel anxiety and panic come over me. I thought about just leaving, but the reality was that I couldn't delay the inevitable much longer, so I hung out with my three new best friends until the girls came out. These were good guys, who talked to me while I waited and even offered me a beer. I couldn't tell you what we talked about since all I could concentrate on was holding it in, and thinking how embarrassing this was. Finally the bathroom door opened and out walked three "hot girls". One of the guys told them that I needed to use the bathroom, which his girlfriend answered "I still have to curl my hair, but you can go in while the curling iron heats up." I thanked her and then quickly entered the restroom, locking the door behind me. I turned on the exhaust fan to help drown out the inevitable noises. I barely got my drawers down when the floodgates opened and what came out would've caused a sewer rat to gag. It sounded like a cappuccino machine and had the same color and texture as the trendy beverage. The whole transaction lasted just 4 or 5 minutes, but it seemed like an eternity. During this time I had an epiphany. I thought to myself, *who cares what these girls think, do they not have bowel movements? Of course they do, and if they can't deal with the fact that this is just a normal part of nature, then that is their problem.* I finished up, flushed, turned off the fan, and walked out of the room with great pride and relief. I felt my confidence fleeting as I made eye contact with the ladies, so I quickly said thanks and briskly walked towards the exit.

Before I made it out of the condo, the girl who still needed to curl her hair started to re-enter the bathroom. As she did, she screamed out, "OH MY GOD, THAT'S DISGUSTING!"

At that moment, my brisk walk turned into a sprint and out the door I ran. After a good distance from the condo I looked back and saw all six of them running outside gagging and coughing. Momma sure would have been proud of me that day.

Chapter 6

Spring Break: The next Day

The next day, my friends and I got up early (Spring Break early is about 10:30 a.m.) and after the hour plus drive, we hit the beach at about 1:00 p.m. The simple combination of drinking a lot of cheap beer and a diet of greasy fast, food cheeseburgers with fries for an entire week spells Trouble. Throw in the fact that our home base was more than an hour away and most stores and restaurants aren't too keen on letting college students use their bathrooms, spells another chapter of Poop Tales. We had been there for a couple hours; walking up and down the beach, drinking beer, laying around and getting some sun, when I felt those all too familiar pangs in my stomach. I fought it for a while and thought I could possibly hold it back a few hours until we get back to our temporary dwellings, where I can really relax and let loose. While lying on a beach towel, I began tossing and turning, trying to find a position that would provide at least a little relief. The sweltering sun made me uncomfortable, inside and out, so I decided to take a dip in the ocean.

I thought that would help by cooling me down and

getting my mind off of the tension. It didn't!! I couldn't take it anymore; this bad boy inside me was touching cloth!! I decided to go out a lit bit deeper, drop my drawers and let it rip. I swam out where there were no other swimmers in the vicinity. So there I was, standing in chest deep water, with my trunks around my ankles, trying not to moan too loud in relief. Since I was so focused on the task at hand, I did not take into account when choosing my location that the water in the ocean rises and falls with each wave. Therefore, the water that had come up to my chest was now only waist deep and getting shallower by the second with the swell of each wave. I stayed the course and proceeded to do deep knee bends to the rhythm of the waves while taking a dump. Once finished, I pulled up my shorts and turned around to view the damage. Wouldn't you know it? It was a floater.

During my intense concentration, I hadn't noticed that my buddies had since joined me in cooling off in the "crystal clear waters" of the Gulf of Mexico. I called out to one of them who was already swimming toward me and said "hey come take a look at this." He nonchalantly wades over to view what I'm sure he thinks is a jellyfish or some other sea creature. My old buddy gets about three feet away and sees the creature which I created. He suddenly recognizes the beast that is not native to these waters and begins to panic. He frantically starts to splash and back pedal, but the slight under tow actually pulls him out to sea. At the same time, the next wave pushes the hideous beast in towards him. He was splashing and screaming like a victim from "Jaws." Somehow, he avoids contact with the floating creature, but to this day he is still afraid to go back into the water.

Chapter 7

Spring Break (The Trilogy)

This story, like the others before, finds me needing to use a bathroom in a bad way, with none available again. It was early evening and we had been driving around the strip, looking at girls. My stomach started its normal churning and turning. I had been partying for five days and the last few sit-downs had me feeling like a root beer dispenser, full of brown, foamy liquid. I could tell that this was going to be a bad one and it was moving in real fast. I told my buddy to pull over at this little strip mall so I could beg one of the storeowners to let me use the facilities. This strip mall was in the shape of a box with the openings being in the corners and the storefronts facing inwards. I ran around from door to door, but all of the stores were closed. Time was running out for me and I had to think of something quick.

This is a Spring break for four college buddies, so our agenda for the night was the same as it had been all week: go to the bars and hook up with some girls. I'm not really what you would call smooth when it comes to picking up women, but even I know that if I poop my pants, I'm pretty much done for the night. (Definitely done with the ladies, but I'd still probably go to the bars after tossing out the boxers). Even if there was a girl out there that would hook up with me after doing that, I'm sure I wouldn't want to hook up with her. I looked around as the sun was setting, for something to spark a plan. I spotted a 55 gallon drum that was located outdoors, in the middle of this mini-outlet mall. The drum was about four feet tall and was being utilized as a trash can. Perfect! Well, good enough. I ran over, dropped my drawers, hopped up and sat on the edge with my rear hanging over and balancing myself with my arms. Now, the only good thing about the urgency of the situation is that this meant the deposit would be quick. Within a minute, my transaction was completed and I was now faced with a new dilemma. I still needed to wipe!

I glanced down from my perch into the trashcan. Everything in there that I could have used to wipe with was now already covered. I couldn't very well just pull up my pants and ignore this important task, or I'd pretty much be in the same creek that I would have wound up in if I'd just pooped my pants, and we all know the name of that creek. I hopped down and pulled my pants up about half way. I proceeded to do the penguin walk/run towards the car and yelled to my extremely sympathetic friends "Hey fellas, quick, pop the hatch!" Through hysteric roars of laughter, I heard the latch click and slowly raise open as I approached. I franticly looked for something, anything that may be soft and absorbent. AH-HAA! "A beach towel!" I exclaimed. My friends were all laughing so hard they could barely stand, except of course for the guy who suddenly realized that I was violating **his** towel. I threw down the towel after a few quick, but thorough wipes, pulled up my pants, hopped into the car and screamed: "GET IN, LET'S GO!" as if I'd just robbed a bank. I was too focused to notice how many people actually had the privilege of seeing my little escapade, but my buddies informed me that I was pretty much in plain view of several cars that had driven by on the main strip. Who knows, if you were in South Padre during the spring of 1990, maybe you were one of the unlucky ones.

Chapter 8

Even the Ladies Doo

"Honey, I don't feel so good, you better just go down without me," my wife says to me as I head downstairs to entertain my parents. My folks are visiting for the weekend because my wife and I had our second daughter just 10 days prior. My mother is extremely excited to see all of us and can hardly contain herself as she is naturally a person full of nervous energy. She isn't here two minutes before she picks up a broom and starts sweeping, or heads to our laundry room to fold clothes. Being a bachelor for several years before getting married, I could care less who folds my underwear just so long as it is not me. But, those wives out there, human enough to read this, I'm pretty sure the last person that you want doing your house work for you is your mother-in-law. Although Mom's overzealous nature can bug the heck out of me, she always means well and is the type of person who would do anything in the world for her family. My Dad is a perfect match for my mother, since he is as cool as they come and when he does break his silence; his words tend to have a calming affect on Mom.

As soon as I enter the living room, I'm bombarded with questions: "what's going on up there?" "Where's Kelly?" "Is she sick?" "Why won't she come down?" "Is she mad at us?" "Should we leave?" I finally get a chance to answer and simply state, "she is fine, she just has a bit of a stomach ache, I'm sure she will be down later."

To put it bluntly, my poor wife has not had a bowl movement since giving birth ten days ago and she is experiencing terrible cramps due to the constipation. My wife indicates that although she has felt the pressure of a bowel movement for several days, the pain and sensitivity from the tearing has prevented her from going. Over the next hour, I've tried sneaking upstairs to check on my wife without notice while my parents are playing with my two daughters, only to be hit with a series of questions from Mom, similar to the ones she has already asked, each time I return. Finally, as I grow inpatient with her questioning, I blurt out "listen Mom, there is nothing wrong, and Kelly is just suffering from severe constipation!"

"Oh" is the only word she utters at this moment. I feel like I just betrayed my wife as I spilled the beans and notice my Dad quietly sitting in the living room, reading the newspaper. A small smirk spreads across his face and his continued silence speaks volumes as if to say: *I told you not to ask questions, Dear.* Then with a tone that sounds as if I'm being blamed for my wife's misery, Mom blurts out "Well, go check on her, No.... wait, run to the store and get her some Ex Lax, that always helps your Dad!"

"Mom, I think she just wants some privacy, ok?" I head upstairs to check on my wife again only to find her curled up on the bathroom floor in obvious discomfort. "I think I'm going to call my doctor," she states. Following her phone conversation with the doctor she informs me that he is recommending a Fleet Enema. She adds, "if that doesn't work, then we'll have to go in to his office where he will have to unpack the colon." Obviously without much thought I respond quickly with dumb, curiosity "you mean he's gonna have to go up in there by hand and dig it out?" My sweet loving bride commands: **"Shut up and get out of here!"**

All my attempts of trying to preserve my wife's privacy are dashed by my Mom's inquiries again. "Where are you going?" "Why is the doctor involved?" "Should I go up there to check on her?"

"Heavens no!" I blurt out. "I'll be back soon."

An hour has passed since my wife has taken the enema and I decide to go up and check on her. My wife is a petite, young woman who barely stands five feet, two inches tall. She is incredibly beautiful and has a rare look that perfectly combines a quirky cute personality with a strikingly pretty face. She is also all about style and elegance from her shoes to her hip hairstyle. She is one of those people who take close to an hour to get ready, just to go to the gym to work out. Therefore it finally hits me, how miserable she must feel, as I looked in and saw her standing up, knees slightly bent, legs spread and leaning against the wall with an old towel underneath her. She is completely naked and terribly strained. Lying below her on the towel are about 7 or 8 tiny little turds that look more like chocolate covered raisins. I couldn't help to wonder if the preacher at our wedding had actually known this moment was coming when he said "for better or for **worse.**" I meekly ask "Honey, do you need anything from me?"

"Get out of here and leave me alone!!" is exactly the answer I was hoping for.

Approximately twenty minutes later while we were downstairs watching television, I hear a few short, faint shrieks of pain from upstairs. I begin to head upstairs in a rush and as I'm half way up I hear a loud sigh/scream followed by a loud thud. The thud, literally sounded, as if someone had just dropped a cantaloupe on the floor. Before I even reached the top of the stairs, I got a whiff of what smelled like a cross between a dead skunk and a backed up septic tank. To my amazement, I happened upon a giant ball of poop that was the size, shape and hardness of a regulation soft ball. My poor petite, little wife was lying on the floor in pure exhaustion with sweat on her forehead. Although the stench was absolutely horrible, I couldn't help but wonder how in the heck did this thing come out of my sweet, little bride. Breathlessly, she asks me to throw it into the toilet for her. As I picked it up with a couple of paper towels, I proceed to say stupid comment number two: "my goodness, it must be a three pounder."

Early next morning I wake to a familiar stench only to walk in and see my wife lying next to another giant sewer rat. Only instead of a round ball, this one was a little less girthy, but made up for it in length as it was about 10 inches long. I preceded with stupid remark #3: "Man, baby, yesterday you threw out the ball and today, you toss out a bat!"

Chapter 9

Office Calls

I have truly entered the world of adulthood when I obtained my first job out of college in a small social service agency that provides services to children who are in foster care. Sure I've worked before, during high school and college, but being professional was never part of the job description when I had a paper route or was delivering pizzas. Although the pay is not much more than those other jobs, I have responsibility as well as a satisfaction that I've never had before. I also have "colleagues", whom a few are my parents' age. I'm surprised to find out that I actually can act mature (keyword is Act).

Our office is always packed with people in the mornings and it typically thins out in the afternoons while most of us work out in the field, unless you're bogged down with paperwork. This morning is even more crowded due to the presence of a guest speaker who is providing training to the entire staff. I work with several wonderful people who have welcomed me to the agency and have made me feel very comfortable as an employee in just a few short months. Although I must admit, feeling comfortable while talking to my colleague

Bill about a date I had over the weekend is one level of comfort, and being able to walk into the unisex restroom and drop a bomb is a completely different level of comfort.

I am a pretty regular guy and the freedom of the job has allowed me to plan on being out in the field when nature is usually scheduled to call. It is about 10:00 a.m. and as I sit in an extremely uncomfortable metal folding chair, I realize that when nature calls this morning, I may have to let it ring. I'm nearly sitting in my neighbor's lap as I feel the need to release some pretty nasty tension. I hate to miss my chance, which inevitably makes me horribly bloated, gassy and nauseous. Even though there are at least one hundred people in the room, the silence is almost unbearable. My stomach begins to wake up about ten people sitting around me. The audible grumbles begin to increase in both frequency and decibels. A lady close to me breaks the embarrassing silence by politely saying, "I'm hungry too." The former pizza delivery guy in me wants to say "Honey, we both know them aint hunger pangs!" Instead, the colleague in me says, "yeah I wish I had brought a little snack." Suddenly a guy behind me reaches out and offers me some of his chili cheese corn chips. *Great, that ought to get rid of my gas problem,* I think to myself. I go along with the charade and take a few crunches, but the crunching is only drowned out by a loud "EEEEEUUUYYYYOOOO!" coming from my stomach. Translation: *you better tell that Ass of yours to let me out nice and easy or I'm gonna blast my way out!*

The speaker finally dismisses us for a mid morning break. Unfortunately everyone is standing and talking around the

34

water cooler, which is right next to the only men's restroom in the building. To make matters worse, it is one of those cheap, balsa-wood doors that is definitely not sound proof. I've often heard trickling in there, which is no comparison to the noise level that the bomb I've got knocking at my backdoor will no doubt let out. I can only imagine how loud the celebratory roar will be, as it dives into the pool, making a big splash. Even if by some small chance there was no noise to be heard, the fumes are sure to creep out, knowing what I ate. But I've got to do something, I'm miserable here.

Think...Think...I got it, "Hey Bill, I'm having a tough time staying awake so I'm gonna run over to the gas station across the street for some coffee, you want anything?" "No, but I'll walk over there with you for some fresh air." *Oh great, I just need to be alone,* I think to myself. I'm able to convince myself as we walk toward the door that he won't think twice about me taking a little extra time in the bathroom, and who cares if he does, he's a guy too. I'm finally feeling confident that relief will be here soon. "Hey guys wait for us" calls out three of the ladies in our office. *Oh perfect, I can't spend ten minutes in the bathroom while they all wait on me, they will surely know what I'm up to in there, or worse yet...when I come out that will remind one of them that they need to go, which is another one of those unisex gas station bathrooms.* Did I mention they are all hot, which shouldn't make a difference but let's be real...it does. Damn, missed my chance again.

I take my seat back in the meeting and begin to feel huge gas bubbles trying to surface. The trainer announces that we will work through lunch to get dismissed a bit earlier, while the caterers are already bringing food to us. I can't catch a break. Finally the conference is over and everyone begins to release to the hall. I'm beginning to feel so uncomfortable that I can hardly take it, which is beginning to overshadow the self-conscious feelings. *Come on you freakin people get back to work,* my thoughts pound in my head so loud they could almost be heard, as I notice everyone socializing around the water cooler again. As I contemplate going in, here comes good ole Harvey. Harvey strolls right by me, pleasantly making his way through a group of people standing by the restroom and heads on in. I've never been so envious of another man in all of my life. Despite the fact that he is about 68 years old and slightly heavy set, I want to be Harvey right now more than anything else in the world. You see, Harvey takes this casual stroll down this hallway every single day in the same manner: carrying a newspaper under one arm and a cup of coffee in the other. He even makes small talk with each and every person on his way toward his Throne. He typically takes twenty minutes or so and there is no doubt what he's doing in there. As a matter of fact I've seen ladies run up and say "Hey Harvey, do you mind if I run in and freshen up before you take care of business?" Harvey is always pleasant and smiles as if he is the big man on campus. He confidently says, "not at all, go right ahead." Everyone in the office jokes about the awful smell that he leaves for us everyday, yet he doesn't seem to mind at all. *Why should I mind? It's a natural, normal body function that we all must do.* As my stomach sends another round of gas bubbles through my colon, I decide to follow Harvey.

I start on a deliberate walk toward the restroom as Harvey comes out. I am about to cross the threshold when the smell hits me. *Damn, that ain't normal...* I chicken out again.

The office has finally cleared out and I'm one of the only people left with the exception of a few who are clear on the other side of the building. The pressure from the gas continues to mount as I'm working on paperwork at my desk. *Maybe if I just lean to the side and let a bubble or two out, I can make it to the end of the day, go home and release the hounds,* I think to myself. I haven't seen anyone in nearly 15 minutes, so it seems safe enough to slide out a large and hopefully silent gas bubble. The relief sets in almost immediately as I successfully make room in my stomach by silently cutting one. Before I can sigh, I feel like somebody is standing right over my shoulder. The soft voice that followed confirmed that I was not alone. I recognize the female voice to be my supervisor and she is leaning over me with her face about six inches from my shoulder. "Hey Jeff, How are things going?" Before I can get out a word to answer, I notice from the corner of my eye, that she stops all motion and in an instant, jerks herself straight up and away from me as if someone had hit her with smelling salts. This smell is far more potent than any smelling salts. The aroma reeks of left over Thanksgiving turkey with a hint of barnyard. My supervisor's eyes begin to water.

Feeling a need to say something, I try with a nervous "can you believe the smell from the bathroom reaches all the way down here?" She curtly answers...."No!" She just walks away without any interest in my answer to her original question.

I can't believe this darn day! I've sat in misery all day long to avoid embarrassment, due to being so overly self-conscious, only to break wind, right in my boss's face. The best I can hope for is that she has some sick sense of humor and decides to handle the embarrassing situation like my college buddies would. By retaliating and planting a nice butt bark about six inches from my nose. Unfortunately I wasn't so lucky, turns out she didn't find it to be funny at all, but had no problem sharing the details of my embarrassing moment with the attractive girls in our office to let them decide for themselves. And of course, they did find it to be quite humorous.

Chapter 10

Unbelievable

My first year of college, filled with feelings that I'm sure most college freshman have. An inner conflict of emotion erupts inside me as independence from my parents is finally obtained, yet overwhelmed by all the decisions before me. I feel excited to be away from home, yet home sick for Mom's cooking at every meal. My new friends are awesome but they aren't my old ones. All the new girls to meet, but.... well, I didn't really see a down side to that one. The one thing I was really missing was being involved in competitive sports and being a part of a team. I was from a small town high school and had always participated in athletics. I had played sports since the little leagues and found myself without a team for the first time in 12 years. I had considered playing football at the large university that I was enrolled in, but they hadn't considered me. I'm not sure if they were hung up on my 165-pound frame or if it was my lack of speed and talent.

A new friend of mine and a "much older, wiser junior" played rugby for the university club team and invited me to give it a try. I hesitated since I really knew very little about the sport except that it seemed like a cross between football and soccer. He told me there was a scrimmage game coming up the next weekend and that I should go with him to watch and see if it might be something I'd be interested in. I went to watch, but the opposing players did not have enough players to play the game. They asked me if I wanted to play, so I reluctantly said yes, but explained to them that I had never seen a match, let alone played before. After about three minutes of instructions and a lot of encouragement, I was in the game. By the end of the first half, I was hooked. After the game, my friend convinced me to come up with the $32.50 for the shorts and the shirt and what do ya know, I'm officially on the Rugby Club.

Being a part of this team was better than any team I'd ever been a part of. They were a great bunch of guys and we went on road trips every weekend to play in various parts of Missouri and Iowa. The more time I spent with these fellas, the more I realized they were absolutely crazy. They would party in the van all the way to the match, drink and smoke during the game and then party with the opposing team after the game. There were never ending stories that were primarily B.S., but it was a lot of fun.

I remember one weekend when we had a tournament in St. Louis that turned out to be a pretty rough one. We had five matches in two days and only won two of them. I had played every minute of every game leaving me exhausted. I was extremely sore on the ride back home and couldn't wait to get back to my dorm room to get some sleep. Although

I was hungry, I would have rather went straight home when someone suggested that we stop at this all you can eat buffet. I was feeling a bit perturbed knowing that "all you can eat" to these guys meant: all a normal person could eat plus three more plates. This would take us at least two hours and use up my last six bucks. I considered staying in the car to sleep, but I really didn't trust these guys to leave some poor sleeping slob alone. Looking back, I am glad I went in because what happened in that restaurant became my best and worst memory of my rugby career.

Everything was pretty normal for the first half hour. The guys were stuffing their faces and telling tall tale after tall tale, with a few new ones from our current weekend's festivities. A couple of the guys got up to head for the restroom, joking that they were going to make some room for another plateful. Both guys had smiles from ear to ear as they returned from the bathroom. One piped up, louder than necessary for our table to hear, "You gotta go take a look in the bathroom, someone left a turd in there that's as big as a 2 Liter soda bottle!" I instinctively looked around the room after his roaring announcement to see the disgusted looks on the faces of several families who appeared to still have on their church clothes. Of course, three guys from our table bolt into the bathroom hollering all the way in, "No way, it can't be that big!" (For college guys, taking a look at a huge brownie log comes in a close second to a wet T-shirt contest) The three guys come back to our table from the restroom with shit-eatin grins on their faces (couldn't help the pun). They too, didn't seem to know what discreet means, as they were hollering out the same proclamation.

That was it! Curiosity had grown larger than the disgust in me, so I too headed to the Can to discredit those idiots. Don't get me wrong; I had no doubt that it was probably a big one, but the girth and length of a 2 Liter bottle, no way! A couple of buddies came in with me and we all ran to a stall to find the Beast. I noticed my designated toilet was empty when I heard a loud "Oh My God!" from the stall on my left. When I made my way to the bowl that held the bounty, I couldn't believe my eyes. For once these guys weren't exaggerating. It was indeed the size of a two-liter bottle. This thing was so big that two thirds of it was sticking out of the water. Of course when we made it back to our table to confirm that this instant legend was in fact as large as had been proclaimed, our table cleared with a rush of about 10 people heading to take a gander. A gentleman at a table close to ours, who must have been in his 70's leaned over to me and said "That's a big one, ain't it?" For the next 20 minutes or so, men young and old from tables all over the restaurant paraded into the crime scene to witness the spectacle that was sure to become legend. There were about two hundred people eating at this large restaurant and word was spreading fast. I realized that looking at gross, disgusting, unbelievable things isn't just a college guy thing; it's a **Guy** Thing.

Now, believe me I really don't expect anyone to believe that a human could ever expel something as large as a 2 Liter bottle from the unmentionable orifice, because if I hadn't seen it, I would have never believed it. This monster may have still been there for you to go and see, since there was no way it was going down without assistance. That's where future employee of the month enters the picture. The entire ruckus forced management to act. A poor unsuspecting employee got up this particular morning; put on his pants the same way he probably does every morning without any warning that he may experience Post Traumatic Stress Disorder from the unfolding events. As we were getting up from the table to go home, we see an employee come out of the kitchen, wearing a long apron and holding a butcher knife in his hand. As the man came back out of the restroom, he appeared a bit pale, but for the most part had been unscathed. That is more than we can say for our 2 Liter buddy as he was now, nowhere to be seen. All that was left of this Beast was the cloudy aftermath swirling in the bowl.

Chapter 11

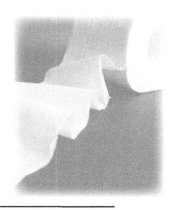

The Boy only a Mother could Love

"Hey, I'm going home this weekend to a party, anybody want to come with me and get a home cooked meal?"

"I will"; "I'm in"; "Road trip baby!" Each of my housemates responds. There is nothing better for a college guy than getting some of my Mom's home cooking, partying with my old high school buddies, and seeing some old girl friends. This should be a great weekend!

As much as I love the freedom of college and all that it entails, I do love going home. Home was where I was King, at least in my own mind. I knew everyone and everyone knew me. To top it off, I had the best of both worlds whenever I went home during a college break. My Mother started to treat me like an adult in some ways as soon as I left home. She allowed me to go out and do as I pleased. The strictly enforced curfew that caused me to go home cold from a hot date on more than one occasion, just a few months prior when I was a high school boy had suddenly disappeared now that I was a college man. But on the flip side, Mom must have been experiencing empty nest syndrome, because she typically took care of me like I was her little boy as soon as I walked in the door. Mom cooked my favorite meals, baked my favorite cookies, did my laundry, and had groceries ready for me to take back to college. She was great! During those days, I really didn't know or appreciate how much Mom really loved me, but as the story unfolds, I will find out just how much.

My friends and I arrived at my mother's house around noon on Saturday. My mom greeted us with the smell of chocolate chip cookies and then proceeded to make us sandwiches before she started our laundry. She didn't just take care of my laundry, but she did all of ours. It must be some kind of code amongst mothers, because all of my friends' Moms would do the same thing for me when I would visit their homes. While she was working on our laundry and preparing dinner, we went outside to play a grown-up game of wiffle ball. Not once did we think about going back inside to help, until we heard that lovely sound "dinner's ready!" We gorged ourselves on a wonderful meal of meatloaf, mashed potatoes, gravy and corn. We expressed our gratitude with sincere compliments as our third and fourth helpings seemed to speak for themselves. Once the food was gone, we proceeded to clean up…. ourselves…we had some partying to do. Of course we offered to do the dishes, but Mom insisted that we relax and have a good time this weekend. I don't think Mom realized, we had a good time every weekend. Still, we didn't want to upset Mom, so we showered and headed out to the party.

We were heading to a country field, where college

age Midwesterners often gather for a "Keg Party." A Keg of beer is typically the premiere choice of beverage for poor college kids. We hung out at the keg party for several hours since we could drink as much as we wanted for one low price. As usual, I over did it! Once we have filled up on liquid rhythm, our designated driver took us to a dance club. It didn't take long for the bouncer at the door to realize my inebriated condition, and wisely turn us away. So, we decided we should probably call it a night.

It was late, my parents were in bed, and all the lights at my house were off. We all thought going to bed sounded like a good idea since some of us needed to get back to school the next day with time to study for Monday's test. Being the gracious host that I am, I let everyone use the bathroom before me. I reminded them to be quiet since Mom's room was right next to the bathroom. I must admit that being nice wasn't the only reason I let them go first, I could feel the beer lubing up that meatloaf for a nice ride down the Poop shoot. It was still working inside of me, so I figured it might take awhile. After my three buddies took their turns, it was finally my turn. I sat down, leaned back to get comfortable... and to tell ya the truth, that's the last thing I remember.

The next morning I awoke in my comfortable bed with the wonderful smell of bacon, eggs and pancakes. My buddies were waking up at the same time and we all headed right to the table. We all sat down to pick up our tableware, when my Mom said to me: "go wash your hands, son." Feeling like I had just been spoken to like a little kid, I tried to laugh it off by saying "come on fellas, she's a stickler on these things." Before anyone got up, she quickly said, "I was just talking to you!" Again feeling like I had just been put in my place, I asked "Why me, Mom?" She responded calmly by stating "because you should always wash your hands after using the restroom." Finally, I felt a bit of redemption, because she had surely misspoken, since I came to the table straight from bed. I confidently answered, "Mom, I didn't use the restroom this morning." To that, she finally looked up from her cooking and looked directly at me with a look that seemed to express a multitude of feelings including a little disappointment, some humor and a bit of disgust. She answered with a tone that revealed she was more humored than anything else, "I believe 2:00 A.M. is considered this morning." My friends' faces lit up and their ears were perked, as they couldn't wait to get any dirt on me that was available.

Mom proceeded to explain, to my friends' great amusement, how she heard me stumble into the bathroom, but never heard me come out. She got up to check on me, but when I didn't respond to her knocks, she opened the door to find her baby boy in all his glory. She found me reclined back, pants around my ankles and a horrid stench that confirmed to her that I had accomplished the goal that had brought me to that room, nearly a half hour before. My so-called buddies were on the floor with laughter, committing every word to memory. They wanted to be sure to be able retell with great accuracy every detail at some future social gathering, no doubt in mixed company. She continued describing the humiliating scene and how she pulled up my pants, flushed the toilet and put me to bed like a two year old. I had to ask: "Did you wipe me?" All she could say was "No way!" Although the chafing was already beginning to kick in from ass rot, I was relieved to hear that she didn't finish the job for me. I knew I'd probably never live this one down, but if she had told my buddies that she wiped me, I'm sure I'd have had to transfer to a new college.

Chapter 12

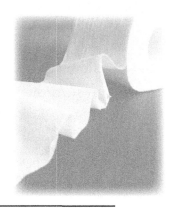

Always Respect the Grumbles

This chapter is not actually about a specific experience, but rather a detailed description of a process that everyone who has ever consumed food, has surely experienced. So take these words as a forewarning to always Respect the Grumbles. What are the Grumbles? I'm sure there are thousands of catch phrases people use to describe the exact same sensation, such as the volcanic colon, the internal tornado, the riot from below or my favorite: The Grumbles. For me, this word actually describes an entire sequence of events that leads to a final upside down volcanic eruption.

The grumbles can vary slightly from person to person, but most of us can certainly identify with the core elements. Whether caused by a viral flu bug or the result of a bad beef and bean burrito, pressure is the key word.

Often times, the beginning of the grumbling tummy is a sudden uneasy feeling that surfaces with a sound of gurgling. One must admit that whenever you're standing next to some poor slob and you hear their stomach gurgle, you can't help but feel relieved that the grumble came from his stomach and not your own, knowing exactly what is to come for this poor unsuspecting bastard. Usually about five minutes pass before the next gurgle is heard. The second grumble is always louder, longer and stronger than the first. The sound causes you to visualize bubbles slowly surfacing in a thick, bubbling oil spill.

The grumbles begin to arrive closer together with greater intensity and the pressure in the stomach begins to shift down toward the pelvis. For whatever the reason, cool air tends to speed up the process for myself. I've had to turn off the air conditioner while driving in 95 degree weather and turn on my heater, just to slow the down the grumbling tides.

At this moment, the grumbling begins to move in even quicker as the pressure begins to build up below the pelvis. All the gas propelling the big boy through the tunnel seems to be honing in on its only way out. The mounting pressure causes sweat to bead off of one's forehead. At this point the goods are beginning to pound at the back door. Huge amounts of gas are building up behind the only muscle that is more important than your heart right now. Expelling a little bit of this gas during the early phase of the grumbling process may buy you a bit more time, but now you don't dare risk it. These farts are no longer funny because they are bringing along plenty of semi-solid friends that are just pounding they're way to sunlight. These waves of pressure sound like I'm describing labor contractions, but despite feeling totally dilated, you don't dare push until you are home free and sitting on top of the porcelain throne. The desperation is upon you as you try clenching, squirming, fidgeting and waddling toward the bathroom. Taking a normal step can be too risky at this stage in the game. At this point, the beast is nearly touching cloth and you only have a few seconds left before the mother load rears its ugly head. The jingling of the belt buckle or the sound of the zipper seems to stimulate the lava much like the conditioning of Pavlov's dogs. At this stage if you haven't made it to the seat yet, then even the largest of men are reduced to what my four-year-old daughter refers to as "The poopy dance." This dance routine is a butt clenching side step and hop from toe to toe. There is some debate as to whether this does anything to slow down the inevitable or just makes us look silly. The end of the grumbles can either be the sweetest relief you've ever felt, or in some cases it could be your most embarrassing moment. Either way, the pressure will soon be gone, one-way or the other.

Chapter 13

I'm Truly Sorry Gas Man

The previous chapter is the perfect description of the series of events leading up to this next tale. The Grumbles set in with a vengeance on a particular trip home from Grandma's house. This may sound like the beginning of a fairy tale, but it felt more like a nightmare. I am the father of two young girls, ages 6 months and 3 and-a-half years. My wife works evenings, so I am proud to say that we split the parenting time of our children, right down the middle. Unfortunately, my wife and I rarely see each other, but it works out perfectly for our girls, as they rarely require a baby sitter.

After several years of being a father, I have no problem putting the baby in a stroller and heading out. I absolutely love spending time with both girls, whether it is going to the park, the grocery store or even a ball game. My identity has changed so much that I've begun to take exception to ladies who frequently ask "Is Daddy babysitting tonight?" I realize they are actually complementing me for taking on a responsibility that has been in the past, typically reserved for the female gender. But, after about three years of being a proud Daddy, I politely respond each time with: "No Mam, these are my kids, therefore I'm parenting!" This response always leads to "yes, yes you are, good for you!"

I have mastered preparing the diaper bag, changing diapers, and taking my 3 and-a-half year old into the gentleman's room during potty training. I pretend I'm a member of a racecar pit-crew whenever I'm in public and I have to change my babies' diaper in seconds flat. This not only entertains my oldest daughter, but it also allows me to see if I can beat my record time. (Guys are easily entertained) The greatest challenge is not what to do when nature calls for one of my daughters, but what to do when nature calls out my name, and I'm out in public without my wife to watch over the kids. I have a great appreciation for those businesses that have taken the initiative to create "family restrooms." For those not familiar with these wonderful facilities, these are restrooms that are equipped with changing tables, a clean stall, a chair and plenty of room for bringing in the kids.

My tale begins at the end of our visit with my grandmother. Grandma lives about 45 minutes from us and she is a widow. I grew up in a home that was located just a short bicycle ride away from my grandparents' house. I spent many weekends at their home. They also included us in a summer vacation every year, which was typically spent in Florida. My brother and I were extremely close to them and I have made sure grandma has gotten to know her great granddaughters. I have developed a routine of driving to grandma's house every Wednesday night after work and having dinner with her and both of my daughters. My girls and I have taken this trip together each week for the past two years. I have wonderful memories of grandma's home cooked meals and she has tried to cook for me on our Wednesday visits. Grandma's age, unfortunately, has affected her ability to prepare these meals, especially over the past six months. Grandma is unable to cook to her own standards but continues to insist that we stay in, rather than go out. I don't have the heart to disagree since the visit is the reason for our getting together, not the meal. Anyone who has a three year old knows the terrible twos don't stop when they turn three; therefore staying in isn't such a sacrifice, even though grandma's cooking has declined a bit. This particular meal however, gave me enough reason to begin insisting that we all go out next time. I have fond memories of the sights, smells and tastes of grandma's lasagna, Italian bread and homemade lemon meringue pie, but tonight's feast found none of those delicacies. Instead, our fare included a can of tuna fish, loads of baked beans and deviled eggs. I did not say a negative word as I took in each helping that grandma scooped onto my plate. I was however, envious of my baby daughter's jar of ham and apples. My three year old had no problems saying "yuck" and was able to get away with the excuse that she had too many snacks on the ride over.

The visit went well despite the eggs, tuna and beans. We said our good-byes and began our journey home. It didn't take long for the grumbles to set in. The ride takes 45 minutes but most of it is through the country with few opportunities for a restroom break. Faced with the dilemma of what to do with the children even if I do make it to the next restroom, since I'm sure, I'm not going to have the luxury of looking for one of those wonderful family restrooms I've described. The tuna and eggs seem to be backing the beans into a corner and they are about to blast they're way out. I have about 5 minutes til blast off, and the nearest gas station is 8 minutes away if I drive the speed limit.

Within 4 minutes, I can see the station, unfortunately though, I can smell the eggs. The gas station is sitting just off the highway near a river. The entrance to the restroom is located on the outside of the building and I realize there is no way I'll be able to make it if I have to go inside to get a key. I also know that I don't have the time to get both girls out of their car seats and bring them in with me. My only chance is to pull up right next to the restroom door and hope it is unlocked. My only consolation is that I have a diaper bag to clean up my mess. The only thing in my favor is that both girls are asleep. I am not comfortable about leaving the girls in the car alone, but I really don't have a choice if I want to drive the remaining 20 miles without sitting in slop. I turn off the engine and lock the girls into the car, just a few feet from the door of the restroom. I reach out for the door handle of the restroom, but it's locked. Oh no! It is starting; uh-oh, I've begun to feel some squirting going on, right in my drawers. I feel like the dyke is about to blow, despite my death clinch. I'm just about to give in to the pressure as I look in the car, directly at the diaper bag and think, *well, I'll just accept defeat, throw the boxers away and use my daughter's wipes.*

Within a split second, the door opens just before I

release the clinching cheeks and out walks a guy who looks a lot more relieved than me. He hands me the key as he walks on by. I head in and get the door shut. I am about to burst when I notice the seat down and there is urine all over it. I felt like running back out and punching that guy in the face, but instead I had no time as I was beginning to leak again. I finally get my pants around my ankles and I grab some toilet paper and began wiping off the seat.

Thar She Blows!!!! While standing, with my rear facing away from the bowl, I feel my sphincter finally give way. If you have ever heard the phrase "projectile vomiting", then you must be able to visualize what my bottom looked like at that moment. I could hear splattering against the wall as I swung around to sit down. By the looks of things from my seated position, it didn't seem to matter now, because the damage appeared to be done. The room looked as if someone filled up a water balloon full of sludge and slammed it against the walls. I could barely keep my lunch down as the foggy stench filled up the room. I could see that I was still going to have to throw away my boxers as originally planned in the "going down without a fight" scenario. I waddled over to the door, still with pants around the ankles to peek outside and check on my girls. They were now waking up. Although they were both still groggy, they were just now realizing that I was not in the car. I stuck my head out the crack of the door so they both could see me. As they made eye contact with me, I could tell they were both a bit concerned. Neither was upset yet, but it was just a matter of seconds until the water works would start flowing.

So I pretended that I was playing peek-a-boo with them in hopes to bring them comfort. It worked, as I had them both rolling with laughter as only my head kept popping out from behind the door and yelling peek-a-boo! Luckily no one was waiting to use the restroom because I can't imagine what someone would have done had anyone have seen some guy's head popping out from behind the restroom door, trying to entertain two small children in a car a few feet away.

In between Peek-a-boos, with pants still around my ankles, I slipped out of my poopy underwear and threw them into the trashcan. I pulled up my pants and washed my hands. I took one last look around the place, contemplated trying to clean it up and decided to get the heck out of Dodge. I left the restroom door unlocked and placed the key in one of the only dry spots on the floor. The girls were still laughing as I got into the car. We slowly drove away from the nightmare that had been mine, but realizing now that the poor guy behind the counter was about to have his own.

Chapter 14

And Yet Another Kid's Tale:

The Newlyweds

One can only imagine the pride felt after having your first child, but to truly understand this feeling, you must actually experience it. I've seen thousands of toddlers and they are all extremely cute and special. But, nothing compares to your own little one. Once my daughter turned two years of age, it seemed that everything she did was ridiculously cute. I mean everything, from her tiny steps to her tiny words to her tiny potty chair. My wife and I were the first couple amongst our friends to experience parenthood; therefore we never can tell when "Sammie stories" have gone from being cute to just plain annoying.

My best friend is an old buddy from my bachelor days. Although he does not have any kids yet, luckily he has just tied the knot recently. This union has bridged our new worlds together. It doesn't take long to figure out how far the two worlds of bachelorhood and married life are apart. The world for a bachelor is Earth. It can be hot, cold but full of life. The marital world for a **male** is much more like the planet Uranus. Uranus is primarily composed of gas, like most men. The temperature is typically at 355 degrees below zero, which is what it feels like when you're in the doghouse. There is a visible ring around Uranus, but no matter how distinguished you become, you'll never be able to stop from being reminded that you are still part anus.

Back to the story! My buddy and his new bride are just beginning to cohabitate and they live in a nice, clean apartment without any pets. He has invited us over for dinner so that these worlds can come back together. My wife has gotten to know my good friend, but hasn't had the opportunity to get to know his new bride, especially since the birth of our own daughter. My buddy and his wife are gracious and patient hosts as they listen to all the "Sammie stories" that they can handle, since that seems to be our primary topic of conversation. Sammie had just begun potty training and despite the fact that we are all still eating, I proudly let everyone know that she has pooped in the toilet for the first time earlier that same day. "Great" is about the only response our hosts can muster up.

Sammie has been extremely well behaved during dinner, which is out of character for any two year old. It doesn't hurt that she has been oooeeed and aahhhed over for the last thirty minutes just for saying words on request such as "Mommy", "Daddy", and "Poopy." Since she was in the middle of potty training, the latter word came up several times. The cuteness factor is multiplied by 10 since she is walking around with big old baggy pants due to the pull-up diapers.

The conversation began to shift to adult conversation, as my friend was finally able to get a word in edgewise to talk about their future. He and his wife mentioned that they hope to build a new home soon as they would like to start a family. We all agree that the apartment is perfect now but it does not have the room needed when adding to their family. The focus of the conversation casually shifted again to how nice the apartment actually was. They live in a two-bedroom apartment that is immaculately well kept. The carpets are spotless and you can't help notice the crisp clean smell of the place. There is no doubt from the looks of this place that they aren't hiding any kids anywhere and that they are definitely newlyweds.

Sammie, who has drifted out of the center piece of the conversation has suddenly stole the spot light back, as she began to run down their hall way toward the restroom, yelling "poopy, poopy, me go poopy!" I've felt like doing the same, on more than one occasion, but I've found out that it is only cute for two year olds. Simultaneously, Sammie whipped down her shorts, kicked them completely off of her leg and started tearing off her pull-up diaper. I suddenly realized that there are times when Sammie forgets the difference between "I **gotta go** poopy" and "I just **went** poopy."

Sammie repeated the little kick move that removed her shorts and was able to send the pull-up diaper flying. We were all quite entertained by all of this action when we all, realized, there was something flying in the opposite direction of the diaper. The thud of a nice, solid chunk of poop landing on the extremely, clean hallway carpet confirmed that all of our eyes weren't playing tricks. The room went completely quiet, as we all watched this little log land and slowly roll to a stop. Sammie never broke her stride as we all watched her little white bum disappear around the corner into the bathroom. She unknowingly sang a victory song as she sat on the throne.

I noticed the stunned looks on everyone's faces since none of us knew what to say. My wife was obviously worried because the apartment was so clean and she hardly knew the new bride. Later we found out that our friends were primarily concerned that we may think they were bothered by all of this and did not want us to be embarrassed. Sensing the anxiety, without fully understanding the dynamics, I decided to break the tension by approaching the little brown beast that had caused such havoc. I leaned over the beast and pointed very closely, without actually touching it and asked, "I don't remember you serving corn tonight." We all enjoyed the laugh including Sammie, who had no idea what was so funny. Laughing is always better when shared, anyway.

Chapter 15

MMMM…MMM! Is that Cider?

The telephone rings and after answering, I hear: "Hello Jeff this is Mom, Why don't you come on over around 3:00 so that you can visit with your grandmother before your cousin arrives." "Sounds like a plan," I reply. My cousin is from San Francisco and is visiting our town on a business trip. I look forward to meeting my cousin for the first time, and of course getting a free, home cooked meal is definitely a perk, since I have recently graduated from college.

I arrive on time to find my grandmother, father and mother visiting in the family room. My grandmother is in her upper seventies and is in good health. Despite her excellent condition, she does have difficulty hearing conversation and her memory is beginning to fade significantly. Grandma can remember every detail about how she and my grandfather met, but she forgets that she has already told this story three times in the last half hour. Grandma is a delightful lady and loves to socialize; therefore she always looks forward to having the family get together. My cousin has not arrived yet, but Mom asks if I would like some Apple Cider. We live in the Midwest and the autumn season is perfect for this warm, delicious treat. This day happens to be a perfect Fall day with the leaves changing, sun shining and a perfect fifty-five degrees outside providing an excellent setting for a cup of hot apple cider with a cinnamon stick.

As I drink my first cup of the season, I can't help myself from drinking it too fast. Although I'm in my twenties, I feel just like a kid who has gulped down his soda way ahead of all the adults before the pizza arrives. My mom notices I'm finished already and says to me "help yourself to another cup." I take her up on the offer and proceed to drink it down just as quickly as the first. I've always been one who tends to go overboard when things taste so well, and this cider is absolutely wonderful. The phone rings and my cousin informs us that she is running a little late and will be over in about 30 minutes. We continue to visit, sip our cider and pass the time waiting for our cousin to arrive. Mom gets up to pour herself a second cup, when she holds up the gallon jug that is about half empty and asks, "Who's been hitting the cider so hard?" I apologize and admit that I have had about four cups in the past hour. "There is no need to apologize, I've got plenty," she adds. We all comment on how wonderful the cider tastes and smells, making for such a nice treat. "You are welcome to have more" as she fills my cup again. "Thanks, I really had forgotten how good this stuff is," I add. Mom replies, "I'd probably drink as much as you have, if this stuff didn't affect my stomach so much."

"What do you mean?" I inquire as I take another gulp.

Dad chimes in, "yeah, I'm the same way, I can't have more than one cup or I get horrible stomach problems." I give them both a hard time and teasingly say, "it must be hell to get old!" We share a laugh and I gulp down the last of my fifth cup of cider. My Dad is laughing as he puts his cup in the sink and asks, "You ready for another?" His voice must have been a signal to my stomach, because at exactly that moment, a loud, whiney grumbling noise yells out from my midsection.

"No, I'm fine" I cautiously answer. "You don't sound fine," he jokes.

My grandmother is hard of hearing but somehow hears the whine from my stomach. Since grandma's hearing has declined, she tends to talk loudly and asks, "What was that noise, did you hear that?" Suddenly, the doorbell rings and I am forced to bend over slightly with a sudden, sharp cramp that seems to have come from nowhere. "Holy crap!" I sigh. My Dad notices my uncomfortable state and just as he reaches for the door to open it for our guest, he laughs out a question to me, "you sure you don't want another cup?" Without missing a beat, he opens the door and greets my cousin. As mentioned previously, I've never met this relative, so once introductions are made, we all sat in the family room to visit. Mom is also enjoying my obvious discomfort, offering our guest some cider and extending the offer to me again. I politely decline, only to have my grandmother pipe in with "what do you mean, Jeff? You love cider" as she insists and prepares a cup for me. Grandma is not doing this to make an attempt at some cruel humor, (which would no doubt be my Dad's motive), but instead is not able to remember that I have already had five cups. I can feel my face turning extremely pale and my forehead is beginning to perspire. My stomach is knotting up like a pretzel.

Everyone is enjoying the conversation, but me, I'm just trying to sit quietly, hoping to sneak under the radar as chaos is running rampid through my insides. Although I'm a guy's guy, I am sure I will never dismiss any woman who is complaining of being bloated and cramping. I'm not sure what Mydol does, but I wouldn't turn it down at this moment if I thought it would give me some relief. My stomach speaks up again with a whiney little growl. Grandma is sitting next to me on the couch and unfortunately she heard it. "What the hell was that noise?" she asks everyone, truly not sure where it came from. Unable to be inconspicuous, I excuse myself to go to the restroom. The pressure and cramps continue to build, but I am unable to pass anything. I can't even seem to let out a tiny bit of gas, which is unusual for me, as I typically have no problem blasting away. After a full 5 minutes of sitting for nothing, I decide to try and slip back into the room. My Dad sees that I'm about to return from down the hallway so he walks over to intercept me and whispers, "You ok?" but with obvious humor in his tone. He adds, "Damn, you are seriously pale and sweating bullets!" The grin on his face definitely confirms that this is not a statement of concern, but rather a point of amusement. I can't actually blame them; I'd be all over this joke if it were somebody else, like one of my siblings. Fortunately for me, none of them are here because any one of them would be needling this to death.

I continue to quietly sit as conversation is all around me. How can I engage in the pleasantries? I am a miserable mess and have thought of leaving on more than one occasion. I have slipped out of the room at least 4 times in the past 45 minutes. I can't move gas or solid out of my bloated, swelling stomach. This is the strangest feeling, I've ever had, as I know something has to give some time or I'm going to explode. The noise in my stomach hasn't stopped its whining and of course grandma notices each time. She also comments each time I return from the bathroom. I'm sure my face would be red with embarrassment if it weren't so pale. Upon my return, my grandma asks, "Where have you been?" My parents take turns wandering into the kitchen to laugh hysterically at my situation each time. I think to myself, how strange I must look to my cousin who is meeting me for the first time. I finally have a breakthrough on my last trip to the restroom, confirming all the action going on in my stomach had some purpose. Although the smell was not near as sweet, the consistency and texture of the substance coming out the bottom end of me looked identical to what went into the top end. I was in the restroom for twenty minutes before returning, only to find my cousin had already left. What an impression I must have made.

As the leaves start to fall from the trees each autumn, the apple cider story always returns. Recently, my parents were telling me about a dinner party they held at their home and were reminded of me when they offered apple cider to their guests. Although my cider experience happened at least two years before, they indicated that they couldn't help laughing when Mom joked to Dad, "I wonder if we should save some of this for Jeff?" They also found themselves quite entertained as they noticed one of the guests seemed to be drinking more than his fare share of this wicked juice. Each of them was laughing hysterically as they re-told the story to me, almost erupting as mom ads "this poor guy must have slipped off to the bathroom at least four times in an hour!" Now you all see where my demented sense of humor comes from. No wonder I eventually wrote Poop Tales, as we all know how the old saying goes: "The apple doesn't fall far from the Tree."

Made in the USA
Monee, IL
14 December 2021

85345894R00049